IN THE SCHOOL OF WORD ENGINEERING

In The School Of Word Engineering

Poems
by
TOMER KLEIN

Adelaide Books
New York / Lisbon
2019

IN THE SCHOOL OF WORD ENGINEERING
Poems
By Tomer Klein

Copyright © by Tomer Klein
Cover design © 2019 Adelaide Books

Published by Adelaide Books, New York / Lisbon
adelaidebooks.org

Editor-in-Chief
Stevan V. Nikolic

All rights reserved. No part of this book may be reproduced in any manner whatsoever without written permission from the author except in the case of brief quotations embodied in critical articles and reviews.

For any information, please address Adelaide Books
at info@adelaidebooks.org
or write to:
Adelaide Books
244 Fifth Ave. Suite D27
New York, NY, 10001

ISBN-10: 1-950437-52-3
ISBN-13: 978-1-950437-52-8

Printed in the United States of America

Contents

Blown letters **11**

Minor harmony **12**

Scoring **13**

moan **14**

rejuvenation **15**

The shortest day of the year **16**

tattooing **17**

A sunny sun **18**

Senses **19**

The Bird of Prey **20**

Diplomatic poetry **21**

Paper **22**

An alliance with a word **23**

Tomer Klein

Hollow Chaos *24*

Cupid of Words *25*

With a strong hand *26*

School of Word Engineering *27*

Dream Science *28*

The chairs game *29*

Hedonism *30*

Murder from red to black *31*

Mathematics *32*

Birth *33*

Venus *34*

silence *35*

String sound *36*

Ambivalence *37*

Poets *38*

Photovoltaic cell *39*

Thirst *40*

In the lion's den *41*

Sun clock *42*

232 degrees Celsius *43*

Singing solo *44*

chase *45*

Haggadah of a song *46*

gloom *47*

Savannah *48*

Harvest words *49*

The Emperor is retired *50*

A bouquet at my feet *51*

Gordian Knot *52*

Beit Midrash *53*

Longing *54*

lotus *55*

tide *56*

as a whirlwind break *57*

The sparks of the wild *58*

Inclusion *59*

breathing *60*

on the beach *61*

silence is hiding *62*

The focus of desire *63*

Abstract art **64**

on guard **65**

shards **66**

moisture **67**

routine **68**

Hyssop and neglection **69**

snow in my city **70**

Breeze **71**

Limerick of sun **72**

sweet baked good with honey **73**

Comet of Will **74**

sukkah **75**

The emotional corner **76**

pattern **77**

Grove **78**

chess **79**

darkness **80**

Restless **81**

Morning Song **82**

A scribe **83**

the eve of a holiday   **84**

Poetic magic   **85**

Game box   **86**

Mind folding   **87**

victory of the spirit over the metal   **88**

The degree of mercy   **89**

Real memory   **90**

afternoon   **91**

cartoons   **92**

Poetic interface   **93**

Seeds of senses   **94**

All this light   **95**

limerick   **96**

sunrise   **97**

Dreaming words   **98**

Mandolins   **99**

About the Author   **101**

Blown letters

Blown letters,
With their weight as a feather,
Are floating slowly
Between rows.
Between drip and gaze
Then they fly
Subordinate,
Justice and fairness
You will call.
As a lot they shall be parted
signs I shall give
Black spots
Lost.

Minor harmony

Sounds disappeared from my heart,
Cheers I'd forgotten
Fell down the throat
Like obscure oppressions.
I broke my notes,
Their taste cracked,
Their contents ran on my lips
Like a thick bone marrow ...
Sensations in my ears
Their voices restless
In minor harmony
Of Gloomy scale
Chords were torn from my body
With a surgical excision,
Smeared, built in my blood,
Connected to a sad symphony
And a song.

Scoring

Dots fall on the paper,
New or old, desired or not,
Like fingers on the table,
Like the dance of rain falling on a window.
The lines now intersect,
Looking for the meaning,
A letter and syllable,
Clustered in ink and chalk,
Their movement is quick,
Their legs are light like elephants,
Their horns rise before me,
Now, too, "Kamatz" and Patach
Crusted light and shadows.
Ink residues remained dotted,
Holam and Shuruk again found their place.

moan

The sea always moaned,
It's the sound that breaks us
In thousands of sweet ripples.
Waves caught up with us,
We got sand in our eyes
Who yearns for quiet

rejuvenation

And we knew rejuvenation with her hands
And silences that seemed to speak
And longing carried on her wings
And emotions that can tell
How we built our Tabernacle.

The shortest day of the year

If the silence longs
Like the Beams of the young moon,
I'll weigh the time
At sundown.
Intersecting shades
Of red and silver
Are filled with each other
In a type of reverse.
On the shortest day of the year
The seconds are elongated
I can feel
The end of the moment
And its rebirth.

tattooing

I love you
Ink droppings filling the skin,
Expressing the words
The message of memory
Written in the heart-shaped box.

A sunny sun

A mealy sun,
Her black spots,
An eternal engine
Of a distant conflagration,
Its earth is scorched,
Its blues burst.
I have changed now,
Maybe
Maybe because
Of electro magnetic interference
Maybe it's heat
which escaped from the shadow?
I was slightly beaten,
My skin is already tired.
Maybe sweating
will cool my pain.

Senses

My ears are screaming,
I was swept away with storm
In a sea of worries.
This whole time,
I searched its darkness.
My fingers are already bleeding
from the damage of thought.
I spoke correctly,
The sound of a net sailing in the wind,
I held the horns of a hall,
Let me die, my disappointments.
I smelled a wildflower,
The darkness sprouted
Suddenly out of me.
I tasted bitter taste
Of success.

The Bird of Prey

You swooped down on me
like a kite on its prey
your claws are sharp and comforting,
your kisses are etching and caressing.
Your touch is like the night's forgetfulness,
for me
your breath is like a prayer
Let's escape
into the depth of the moment

Diplomatic poetry

The heart murmurs
They do not come just like that.
They break out carefully,
Rushing,
Fill four cubits
Of Paper
In a foam
the art of possibility.

Paper

I have a dark and subjected paper
Sharing my life
Long since it was torn.
The words
Sharing fate, being abandoned,
Hugging its lines,
gives him wind,
Until it became an origami ship.
Time gave it thoughts
Longing for my notebook.

An alliance with a word

A word
in its essence
a cutting and deep meaning
in the living flesh of the
page
Its bookmarks are heavy
From constant touches of quill
From the days
I was picking ideas
In the sieve of Refinement
My mind is easy
On the trigger of ink
Twitch of the casing
My shell has been cracked
The breathing shifts
With the stroke of a smile
Burst suddenly
From the darkness of screen

Hollow Chaos

Hollow chaos,
The Thought is already hollow,
I succumbed to the sweetness
Of Pre-bearning phase.
I burned at the hearth of the keys,
The moments tickle with rage,
Thin fingers
Turned to empty seconds
I am Losing the transcript,
My mind has been tainted.

Cupid of Words

My thoughts are dripping,
Plays me like a string,
And I,
An arrow of love,
Shivers from a treading sound.
Although it all
I am writing.

With a strong hand

A beautifully trilled sound
Trembled to a Levantine rhythm,
They were wrapped in the scent of myrrh and jasmine.
I was crowned for you,
From India to Kush to govern
And my moon and my sun turned round
to seven stars of glory.
Signs and wonders I called thy.

School of Word Engineering

In School of Word Engineering
I am an engineer of
Broken words,
Half sentences
And fragments of dreams.
My eyes are out
They have a grip
The basis of the idea
Which contains thresholds
Of thoughts
In the narrow distance
Between heart and screen.
My palm
It's a bridge
Over
The flood,
And my poem
a dam.

Dream Science

A pharmacist with a tongue I dispense potions of
In the wakefulness lab
On the border layer
Between twilight
and darkness.
I capture moments
in sparks of the first
star
letter to letter
I break as the light
At the paper prism
I have no education
In the dream sciences.
my thoughts arise
while I am awake.

The chairs game

Empty chairs on a roof
I gathered as a circle
Alternately attached.
My thoughts are running around
in the clock direction and against
Looking for a foothold
Like a lost Dial.
When the music stops,
One is always lost,
Blooming like a soap bubble
To the memory limbo.

Hedonism

Below zero
There are only worries,
Everything else froze
In the hedonic layer.
If I defrost
In the spring of my mind,
Then there is a rebirth
For the budding of emotion.

Murder from red to black

Between the walls of creation
I shackled my soul
In steel Chains
Of memory.
I turned words
With my fingers
bloodied from a struggle,
Letters broke through
the gaps,
Mixing ink with life fluid
that blackened from Reluctance
Red-hot sentences
Washed over the paper,
Sliding the iron wires.
In a shattering of desires
Sparks burn my skin
as a burnt offering
On the altar of the Poem.

Mathematics

In the blessed mathematics of signs
I wing an equation
without variables
to unify fonts
In a matrix of life.
The thought is not linear,
But maybe it's still possible
converting to another scale
Where desires are continuous.
Maybe then I will find
a solution.
Q.E.D.

Birth

Constrained energy in me
like a can of shaken drink
and I am,
Looking forward to hearing
the blessed sound
of a snap
And the symphony of emotions comes
The words would burst
As an Amniotic fluid from a uterus.
the arrival of pain
will not be long.

Venus

clapping
stop,
A deafening noise,
Explosion of a moment.
My ears are having Tinnitus
From the shock of the battle of thoughts
I nosed the infinity
like a blood fi led abscess
My feet touched
The ground
like the creative hand in Botticelli's painting,
Creating love.

silence

I accumulated silences
One by one,
Cleanly polished,
before the people
In the Display window of the soul.
I chose silences
One by one,
As a white, bright Persian rise.
I set down in the pot of thought
And I stirred.
As useless letters
The silences were born to shout,
Like the whistle of a kettle
On the stove of emotion.

String sound

String sound
In a minor amplitude
Is produced in the furnace
Of moments of disappointment.
The tremors of the body touched me,
Because forever
My soul is the gift of His grace.
On the threshold of silence
I screamed like a dragon,
A quiet creation
of a royal burning.

Ambivalence

For each wavelength
the visible spectrum and beyond
Painting a mirror
In a range of vividness.
Within sight
And to width the spectrum
I collide as a particle
Radiate as a string.
Now I'm dual
My light interferes and breaks
on the spot.

Poets

Poets compute backwards their end
Dream of word that had ceased to be
Dispense dreams the were set in writing
Running away from themselves and touching the root.
Poets are halted between two opinions
Are heretics to the known and despise the untasteful
Carrying on their backs the journey of the world,
Day and night, they put their lives in their hands
Poets take responsibility for truth,
Go to a holyday on their own in a vacation from themselves,
Take a deep breath
And sit down
To write their thoughts in vain ignorance.

Photovoltaic cell

A stimulating thought
My soul as radiation,
Shaking memories
To an exciting situation.
Blinking letters
To the face of recognition,
They brightly lit
My poem.

Thirst

I do not speak high tongue
Just records my history
In broken letters,
In shattered words,
In sentences
That the time humanizes
I do not sing to the wind,
Just creates a
Tone of liveliness
melodies, like fallen leaves
From my heart
Worthy notes
Looking for meaning.
I am not a poet, and in general
The words, obviously,
Lacks Inspiration
When they fell on the banks of a failed stream
I found,
Thus, I believe…

In the lion's den

Hidden light
escaped from the shadow
distillate a desiring soul
In a shivering, painful Temple.
An old mausoleum, half smashed
the outlines have become so serrated
That they resembled a lion's pharynx.
And I'm like Daniel
Dreaming and solving
The mysteries of the heart.

Sun clock

Sun clock -
Its shadow is elusive,
Asking to be precise
Between gaze and a gaze.
it turns on its axis
but remains in its place,
Because the hot sun rays
are a comfort to him.
Another minute, another moment
A magical night would then fly y,
And the dose of the clock will be revealed,
The darkness of his moments will fill
his sleep
in anticipation for morning.

232 degrees Celsius

it was a delight
to burn moments
as elusive paper chips
Flying overhead.
In a blaze of flame
I signed the time
Or
The beginning of his re-creation,
And I got out of it reading
Quietly.

Singing solo

For even if my strength is exhausted,
I shall not remove a scream from my heart,
I will not barrier the
Touch the world
And his spinning blade
Like a double-edged sword
At the Gates of my garden
For even if my strength is exhausted,
I shall not decrease a thought from my mind,
Do not subtract a pulse in my watch.
Like a lost metronome
Which tick in syncope
Unrequited harmony.
For if my strength is indeed over,
I'll conduct the chorus
Of the worries while singing A cappella,
And I'm a single crowd
To myself...

chase

my hidden poetry
was dropped out of sight,
converged upon itself
as a newborn snail,
As if sinking into
A black hole
Of the subconscious.
My fringed poetry
ran away as an Antelope
And I'm a cheetah
In an endless pursuit:
After Elusive
words
Their legs are light
Like hinds let loose
And she did not know that it
Came to me in a flash
And spread her mouth.

Haggadah of a song

A picture and sounds I bounded
as Passover, matza and maror
As I sit down to the Shulchan Aruch
In letter delicacy,
A temple of devoid hands
Towards action.
I did not take a supply of words for the road,
And my idea has unleavened as bread
A matzah cake of memory I carried
To the destruction of thought
parting
The waves of the soul.

gloom

On a bright day
On the edge of a storm
I found myself glooming
Thick with stones
clouds in a potter's wheel.
And I'm like a pale sun,
Trying to decorate colorful scenery
Beyond the cloud,
but get no shard of reward.

Savannah

A herd of words walked slowly
In Savannah of the memory
Between synapses of baobab trees
Whose roots are washed
To a rough heart.
A Herd of words
Scorched with thirst
parked, on the edge of inspiration lake,
sipped eagerly
Liquid thoughts,
Rare muse drops,
In the wilderness of creation.
A herd of words had now settled into sentence,
His legs tapped weight and rhythm,
Structure and motif were held
To the page,
A multitude of colors were desecrated
The parade.

Harvest words

Twilight
I was short sighted
Chips of thought
Moving in the Holy Spirit.
In a silo of words
I applied an idea
For seven dry years.

The Emperor is retired

My eyes are tired from wars.
For years I have been
Crossing in my heart
a raging Rubicon
Of tears.
If I can
Recycle sword blows
For sparks of poetry,
Then I rest alone
Under my vine and under my fig-tree
On my laurels.

A bouquet at my feet

Flowers stamped
As coins that came out
Of the cycle were
Scattered over broken earth,
A bouquet at my feet.
Marble and cold metal
were as piles in my heart
To establish
The pillars
of my life.

Gordian Knot

with a threat of the sword
I broke my breath
to basic precipitation.
I differentiate myself
From the world,
Seeking ripples,
Blowing waves,
Breaking the Abyss
And renews as I choose.
At the sound of a
middle of sea cry
I shall immortalize my moment
In iron letters
On the thicket of my heart.

Beit Midrash

A grey kiss on my forehead
A crown decorated with cries and thorns
As if I were daydreaming.
Melodies of divided realm

*

On the threshold of the
curtain of the ark
I breathed
The sanctity of moments
And sounds of comfort.

Longing

Strumming longing for the strings,
A dull sound of oblivion,
My fingers are already hurting
Burning from a sea of mercy
For which I exhaled
A yell.
Strumming a gaze at the strings of ships,
The horizon emerges slowly,
My eyes are already scorched
From a weeping sun potion
A drop of saltwater
On my cheek
left her mark.
Strumming colors on the sol strings,
Her beams consoled my being,
And when the ball of fire disappears
Into the depths,
I'll return to your bed -
An anchor to the poetry of my life

lotus

On the edge of a lake I drank
Light blue water and awe
Desolation of sweet Water Lilies
Floating in their silence.
I breathed in depth
A moment of lust
Petals for my poems
motioned me to touch.
On the edge of madness
I held a gaze
But in the dead of day
I was crowned as narcissus
To be the governor of the marsh.

tide

Your moon brought my pride,
But my ship is still mild,
Tightly tied
To the thresholds.
On the watershed line
My river who as a whole
led my ripples to your doorway
and with a flush filled my sun.

as a whirlwind break

The tremor getting higher
On the edge of a smug lake,
a whirlwind break
I was caught in the eye of oblivion.
A glance was beating
I held memories
In a lightning rod
The heart chambers filled
with storm.

The sparks of the wild

At the junction point
I was tired of seeing
The sparks of the wild
In my civilized world.
My fancies were dripping
Venom and fear,
Like a wax for deaf ears
Scorched to tattoo
On the skin of a drum
lament by a shout.
My knuckles crack,
Squealing like a door in a storm,
My hands are already holding
In both options
and I am passing unwillingly
On Mine anger and of My fury.
The scent of memory rose,
Planted in a land that is not sown
paves within the way of deeds.
I had a taste of drunkenness,
Did I dream or was I disappointed?
I did not choose you My notebook,
Your sounds are written slowly.

Inclusion

I will not stop
To kill the leaflets of my poems
Petiole and prey words
Wrinkle from my fingers,
blush from wonder.
I will not stop Shedding
Skin and scales of thought,
Hump of letters
I'll cut from young age
an abscess of ink
I will drain from my painfull
Soul.
Then out of a dream perhaps
I will Gather the Tashlich
From a salty hubris concoction
And I'll redeem it myself
for life.

breathing

The air was infected with screaming
Choking particles of thought
As dust they were,
Sparkling against the light of creation.
The blood is still on my lips,
Its color is dark,
Black as fear
While I was a blaze, in this wondrous redness,
I hit the iron of my hand
Until my fingers were flat,
looked like a biscuit.
I dug a step forward and backward
With a fountain pen from the source of my sitting
I was electrified
by the sight of living letters,
I breathed in deeply
Words,
I exhaled
Sentences.
There's nothing like being in my room
with a chorus.

on the beach

Cracked mirror,
Her reflection is sun washed.
On my arm is a single-stringed harp,
Silence flows
carried on a wave tomorrow.
In my mind I lay on a cloud
Like soft cotton, long ago
That I was still tuned
In a range of memories.
Blessing upon my hand
The palm of your loving hand,
Support for my troubles.
On the sands of my death,
My body was a little burned,
A whole sea on my body, I brought
A coin in exchange for your smile and gaze.

silence is hiding

silence is hiding
In the heart of all living
It originates in the angst of desires.
My eyes are on my back
The memory of wondering
As a Galapagos tortoise,
The outline
Evidence of his thinking.
silence is hiding
On the border of desires,
A thin aspiration as a thread
Tears on the thorn of Yod.

The focus of desire

Words as a butterfly fluttered,
A terrible delicacy is quiet in the straits,
Her scent was like a spring that was silent
From the fear of snows,
froze as a pillar.
On their destruction, I shall verify the souls
Deep breathing will create an illusion,
And when comfort comes, I will raise my prestige
On the focus of desire,
My passion a bonfire.

Abstract art

weighed a smile in a coin
Bright Star
In the darkness of the nights,
But your eyes
cannot be quantified
it is abstract as Kandinsky,
Infinite as Escher.
When I get its essence
Only at the corner of my eyelids,
I shall empty my thought
And touch.

on guard

on my gourd
Days and a river
I'll sail down
on the trail of snake,
I'll conjure up
My eyes from seeing
A soft breath
Her silence peeps out.
on a gourd
my nights hold
the wing of my ship,
My sail is still tense,
my anchor beside me.

shards

shards are pulled
From my body as mercury,
Creators on my lips
Puddle of Genesis,
The fluid of creation
staining my pain
Sucking his strength
from the flint of thought.
The heart of the ink incinerator
held my wings,
Burned with flame,
died in my blood
as corrosive blade.
And I am young lamb
Trapped in a bush of discussion
Between me and myself.

moisture

the eastern wind is raging upon mu face
dry breaths destroy my thoughts
I flatter myself furiously
to keep my lips from a quarrel.
The east wind burned my eyes
In a diversity of lost letters, and silence
since the early ages there was moisture
but now it is gone
now in a forgotten place
disappeared.
only droplets sweated my body
to slake my skin from the plowing of tears
to cool imprisoned memories
in a canister for happiness
the sentences shall finally attach

routine

In a daily routine
My thoughts are darting,
Wondering why,
Between Holy and mundane
Sanctifying the possible,
Longing for tomorrow,
But, in fact,
Whether I want to or not,
they are forbidden and permitted.

*

In routine
I am usually blooming
as a squill after first rain
But when the spark of madness
come in as a guest
I'm always more productive.

Hyssop and neglection

I am hyssop and neglected
the patina of my foliage is straight
I am tied with bond
To the seawall
My pupils blink before
The decline of the West.
My skin is turbid
Scorched with the blood of the depth
I breathed in vanity and fear.
vapors condensate on the glass of grace,
the mirror of my soul caught
Spark and thought.
On the border layer
I separate brightness and darkness,
Catching a gaze and return.
in the sweetness if hallucination
two hearts hold slowly.

snow in my city

A string tangles to a circle
Stretched along the avenue of memory.
Trees-trees of thoughts
Glowing in their glory,
Sparkling as Christmas,
They are heavily weighted
My life is like the jewelry of time.
Spreading myself on a shelf
With the knife of exposure
Sharp as a razor blade,
Pages as blue as deep sea
Spread out as the holiday meal.
And I catch a moment
In a snow globe,
my flakes are shaken neatly.

Breeze

a storm
stepped into the drawer,
Letters were devoured like ships of
Cargo and voyage
Into the darkness of the depths of oblivion
With a twirl of eyes and a mirror.

Limerick of sun

Touching and wailing his Beams,
Light to the sun-inclined skin,
humble hiding in his clouds,
The splash of his whispers would break through freckle
the moon shall moan as last night.

sweet baked good with honey

Sweet baked was my poem
Dripping honey at the angles
words were mumbled in the corner
His ribs arched as Honi ha-M'agel
And on the edge of the circle, you say,
Crushed just a little more and be focused
Wave to wave will kiss the tiara
To infinity I shall rise like a shepherd.

Comet of Will

A desire comet rose through heaven,
Shines asynchronously
Hidden at the corners.
And the tear is like polarized glass
Begins to influence,
And I divide and conquer it after devide.

sukkah

I set up my sukkah
In the backyard
between my body being the sun
And between the washing of my soul
in the nile of
The Prayer of the Stars.
my lattice crusted tendons
Wounded and stricken,
Kisses like memories
Peeled from somewhere.
I have removed all sorts of hardships
In a fluid of life that is transparent in its viscosity,
I peeled off my pain
With an exposed nail,
Touches of hamra soil
filled my fingers
as panful thick crumbs.
I painted her branches in layers of repression,
Four hundred microns
Of compressing feelings between the layers,
my limbs are already galvanized
From the ravages of wind and time.

The emotional corner

I put feelings in the corner of the room,
They are hidden in a corner of an attic
shadow of shadows of memories in herd
Buried alive in the abyss.
I will only find a single lifeline
In the dream of the lips, in the vision of a gaze
Emerging from my pockets of traveling clothes
Which instantly turns into a Sabbath cover.

pattern

I poured hours into the days
In a pattern that warms in advance
There are countless virtues and praise.
I poured moments into the pillars of the Temple and will,
Clocks ticking, its circle uncertain
The necessity of my state that is still and silent.

Grove

My pillow silences the evening bed,
Her mouth sipping tunes and tears,
To the kinship she takes a sadly misty cloud,
As a sword he fell with a whisper to the chamber.
In the bed of blankets my gladness shell rise
Head up to a ship of bedding
And in a minaret, I'll find out
The scream of hearts in the silence of lovers.

chess

Sometimes I wander with myself
Between isolated walls that are thought-dependent
Woven as a chessboard,
Slots from nowhere.
As a pawn in my hand I will find my soul,
Black and white merge into one,
I shall ride as a Bishop on kings' road
Into the comforting embrace of the end of the game.

darkness

An inner darkness, a gray shadow,
Ran away from himself long since it was over,
Its edges dim, its heart divided,
Slowing its pace between desirable and found.
Darkness on the edge of a caressing lake,
The wave of the soul breaks, bends and rushes,
Licking rocks of thought, like grumbling,
Noises, dripping, signs in it.
there is upper darkness and lower darkness
the heavens separate them
to crown and conquer
Beyond the pick
strikes like a wave.

Restless

His face was slack,
His breath was like forgetfulness,
His eyelids glide on a blanket
In the thermal column of rest.

Morning Song

as she wakes on the morrow
Her gaze immediately lifted up,
A spark of electricity in a curious eye
Stretching like a naughty spring curl.
In a flash it leaves me devastated,
A storm of a girl swept my heart,
Filled the space.

A scribe

Singing in the dark,
Its touch soft as a feather,
Slowly sinking, rocking
In the harmony of my home prayer.
Poetry stuck to my words
As an artificial claw on my finger.
in silver I scratch the depth of my neck
Runes of weekday and of Sabbath.
I am sanctified in the blood of signs,
Adhesive fabric,
On the doorstep
The mezuzah of letters,
Parchment sealed with candle wax
On a lintel of light bulbs.

the eve of a holiday

I sanctify my moment,
Washed by the times,
On the eve of a holiday,
The story of signs is blessed on her bed.
I am bound to a life forgotten
Like chairs to the Shulchan Aruch correlations,
they are hidden in a cloak of concealment,
praise stolen words
At a time of heavenly mercy.

Poetic magic

Poetic magic is taking shape
In a cracked bowl,
Chopped to show off my skin,
A small fire of desire.
And I am a wimp of words
Adds a wealth of escape elements,
Points and punctuation marks
Preserved in formalin somewhere
Subconsciously.
And to remove any doubts
It tastes like the blood of deeds.
Metallic glued to my tongue,
My lips mingle with mischief.

Game box

In the playground I packed breaths,
A vapor of breath, a choking vapor, shards of dust and thought
Fold neatly, wrapped in cellophane
In a variety of shades and love.
I put down the memory package
On the shelf of oblivion,
Where the waves of time are spinning,
Create a bubble environment
In the texture of space and imagination.
a point of failure in my life
Glued to my ship
Like a sweet, anchore
His rattle reminds me of
Live Clock.

Mind folding

I turned my heart into an origami swan,
His wings are drooping but his neck is borne,
Memory dangling in its folds was stamped.
My legs and my head are buried in the grains of wandering,
My stomach is exposed and restrained by the labor of thought,
As if I were a folding chair,
It was forgotten in the evening
The landing of rescue flags.
But my words as a fragrant laundry were,
Fold neatly,
Organized on a thought shelf,
Soft and comforting
As a baby after bathing,
Ready to wear.

victory of the spirit over the metal

my quill pen like a sledgehammer flies
Pounding in my shining body with redness,
My fingers soot in the air
charred, letters from the ember.
Like small swivel cleaners
assembled at my doorstep signs and verses,
They lay like crushed tastes
Black spots lost.
on the potter's wheel I designed
A quick and intricate piece of work,
And in the movement of pliers from machetes
I gathered with my bare hand
A white-hot iron word.
My tongue stuck to the line,
Tattooing her with a sign like a corrosive acid.
I dropped a phrase
With a cool welcome,
I shall ornament my nose
wreath of testimony as a souvenir.

The degree of mercy

At the edges of the edges gives way
The simplicity of the circle,
I gathered a silence in a hoop
Then I added a thought
Who followed me on the defensive,
Clanging with a flourish
My words are correct and defiant.
One footage to me is clear,
Her deeds are wondrous and merciful
And in the eyes of cure
Under the viewing soul
I passed a rainbow of broken memories
Between sea and cloud.

Real memory

True memory comes from a distance,
Carrying on the wings of flickering silences
Like the labyrinth of life embedded in the rock,
fossilized forever to forgotten.
The real memory is reprinted with a copper
Signs on my glittering face,
The steps of the nail are painted like a brush,
Create an impressionistic moment in people's eyes.
The true memory is sealed with the trunk of the heart,
Rounded from one end to the other
They gather outside with the fleeing hours,
point to point connect to infinity.
The memory is captive to the point of view,
Shackled with cables of selectivity,
A pilgrimage to my thoughts
As the Molech his innocence is sacrificed.

afternoon

Among the twilights
Sending a bare nail between the moments,
swift deer bright horns,
Skipping the edge of an abyss.
pure sheep,
Are counted at a breathing rate,
In the thicket of the quilt they scattered,
That freedom has become,
Words are archived on a page.

cartoons

Cartoons on the radio
And I will stretch the length of the avenue
As a flat figure on the floor of the car,
And the seconds run away from me
As birds of smug paper
above disappears
Sun rays are liars
pink stripes
Cut a guitar sound from the drum,
A slight tremor on the accelerator,
Glass butterflies inside the heart
Like a turning stone
Sowing moments
And a song.

Poetic interface

The occasional touches fluttered like a honey bird
Sucked honey-life as a spoonful.
In my exchanges of grey conversations,
Caressing with my breath.

My chronicles are written with a click,
Fingers kiss on the edge of the keyboard,
Poetic interface was iron lung
Catheter moments in the day of no birth.

Seeds of senses

In the face of time and movement my instincts fell,
Sparks of thought fluttered like kisses,
They left word prints on their arrival
Like sizzling brushstrokes in a forgotten life.

The sound roller shuddered the forearm of the lips
Like a stamp of letters that had left service in the days of silence.

All this light

All this light broke
In pieces,
Conical thoughts
Infertility
In a duality of emotion and compassion.

limerick

On the murky look I will shatter the silence of the storm,
Silver in the words of the crescent moon
Wolves besieging fallen shrines
Singing entire moons,
I'll have the moon for her until the razor arrives.

sunrise

Sunrise whispers puffed up on my face,
Horns are streaming to fear of turmoil,
Morning call with melodies
drummed tiny sticks of light on my lips.
Between the slits of my eyelids
Reveals the creation of thought in a word,
And be good to me
two times over.

Dreaming words

Dreaming words on a page,
Taps of meaning fly by,
Black spots of the subconscious
Pulling out of the field drawers,
But the Palace of Memory is collapsing at the edges,
And I, as Samson cries out to my sweethearts,
Takes me to the abyss of inspiration
The days of my desire in the mirror of creation.
I'll die with words.

Mandolins

The mandolin cuts the heart,
their music struggled with the remnants of wishes,
Carrying their dust against the pale sun,
A journey of roots beyond emotion.
Not a single word was uttered in vain,
Respiratory seizures were cut off in stone from last night,
And we are lucid and clear,
Tattooing the melodies, we chose,
Scorched with terror, but still happy
We were experiencing ghost melodies, loves and silences.
Just like that, as if we were daydreaming,
I knew what you told the soul.

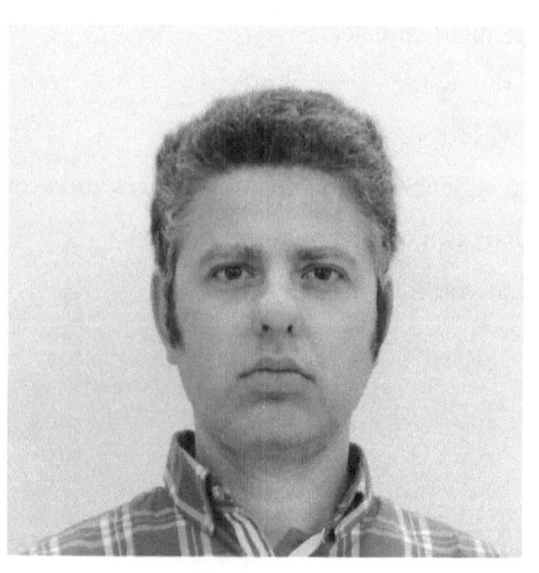

About the Author

Tomer Klein was born on September 27th, 1977, in Haifa, Israel, to Shlomit (a social worker) and Robi (a retail manager). He is the oldest of three (he has one sister and one brother) and he was raised in Akko (Acre). He majored in physics and chemistry during high school.

Tomer was a scout cadet for 5 years. In addition, Tomer played Baritone in Acre city orchestra for 6 years. As a part of an excellence program at high school he participated in several courses. Among those he participated in a photography class for 3 years. Later, during his undergraduate studies, Tomer gave photography classes to elementary school pupils.

Tomer served in the IDF (Israeli defense force) for 3 years, as a combatant in the artillery force. He was released as sergeant first class. He continues to do reserve duty upon request as sergeant major in a draft unit.

Tomer holds a B.Sc. in Chemical engineering (industrial tract) from Ben-Gurion University in Beer-Sheva. His undergraduate research project was done in the Dead sea works potassium plant. The research focused on the topic of crystal size distribution and methods to control predefined sizes. It was the first time this topic was explored in real industrial crystallizer setting. During his studies Tomer worked in ICL (Israel

Chemicals Ltd.) and got a one-year scholarship to map their utility plant. He also volunteered with children from underprivileged families and helped them with social interactions and study enhancement for 3 years.

Tomer worked for various companies in several domains (pharma, chemical industry and cleantech). In recent years he specializes in water treatment and works as an independent freelancer. He designs desalination and wastewater treatment systems. He works with global companies and was involved in projects worldwide. Tomer is married to Dorit (an electrical engineer) and has two children Shir, (daughter, 10 years old) and Yoav (son, 7 years old). He lives in Haifa since 2007. In his free time Tomer likes to read science fiction and fantasy books, watch TV series, attend rock concerts, spend time with his family and of course writing.

Tomer published two poetry books in Hebrew and continues to write and publish on social media and forums. He also provides guidance for young poets in editing and publishing.

Tomer started writing when he was 18 years old and started publishing on forums at the age of 22. His first book ("How sweet to die in the sea", Steimazky publishing house) was published in 2013. His second book ("In the school of word engineering", Niv books) was published in 2018. Tomer writes in modern style, mostly without rhymes. His main topics are Ars Poetica, nature and love.

www.ingramcontent.com/pod-product-compliance
Lightning Source LLC
Chambersburg PA
CBHW020125130526
44591CB00032B/525